Sarah H. Power Whitman

Edgar Poe and his Critics

Sarah H. Power Whitman

Edgar Poe and his Critics

ISBN/EAN: 9783743336254

Manufactured in Europe, USA, Canada, Australia, Japa

Cover: Foto ©Thomas Meinert / pixelio.de

Manufactured and distributed by brebook publishing software
(www.brebook.com)

Sarah H. Power Whitman

Edgar Poe and his Critics

PREFACE.

———o———

DR. GRISWOLD's Memoir of Edgar Poe has been extensively read and circulated; its perverted facts and baseless assumptions have been adopted into every subsequent memoir and notice of the poet, and have been translated into many languages. For ten years this great wrong to the dead has passed unchallenged and unrebuked.

It has been assumed by a recent English critic, that "Edgar Poe had no friends." As an index to a more equitable and intelligible theory of the idiosyncrasies of his life, and as an earnest protest against the spirit of Dr. Griswold's unjust memoir, these pages are submitted to his more candid readers and critics by

ONE OF HIS FRIENDS.

·Edgar Poe and his Critics.

THE author of the "Original Memoir" prefixed to the volume of Poe's Illustrated Poems, recently published by Redfield, says, "Of all the poets, whose lives have been a puzzle and a mystery to the world, there is not one more difficult to be understood than Edgar Allan Poe." The Rev. George Gilfillan, in his very imaginative portraiture of the poet, admits that the moral anatomists who have met and wondered over his life, have given up all attempts at dissection and diagnosis, turning away with the solemnly whispered warning to the world, and especially to its more brilliant and gifted intellects, " Beware ! "

2

He confesses that a history so strange as that of
Edgar Poe should prompt us to new and more search-
ing methods of critical as well as moral analysis. But
before such analysis can be instituted¯we must have
fuller, more dispassionate, and more authentic records
of the phenomena to be analysed. The well written,
but very brief memoir prefixed to the Illustrated Poems,
and the various sketches that have, from time to time,
appeared in the French and English periodicals, are all
based on the narrative of Dr. Griswold, a narrative
notoriously deficient in the great essentials of candor
and authenticity. " It is a rare accomplishment," says
one of our most original writers, " to hear a story as it
is told ; still rarer to remember it as heard, and rarest
of all *to tell it as it is remembered."*

If Dr. Griswold's Memoir of Edgar Poe betrays the
want of any, or *all*, of these accomplishments—if its
remorseless violations of the trust confided to him are
such as to make the unhallowed act of Trelawney
towards the enshrouded form of the dead Byron seem

guiltless in comparison, we must nevertheless endeavour to remember that the memorialist, himself, now claims from us that tender grace of charity that he was unwilling, or unable, to accord to the man who trusted him as a friend.

It is not our purpose at present specially to review Dr. Griswold's numerous misrepresentations, and misstatements. Some of the more injurious of these anecdotes were disproved, during the life of Dr. Griswold, in the New York Tribune, and other leading journals, without eliciting from him any public statement in explanation or apology. Quite recently we have had, through the columns of the Home Journal, the refutation of another calumnious story, which for ten years has been going the rounds of the English and American periodicals.

We have authority for stating that many of the disgraceful anecdotes, so industriously collected by Dr. Griswold, are utterly fabulous, while others are perversions of the truth, more injurious in their effects than

unmitigated fiction. But, as we have said, it is not
our purpose at present to revert to these. We propose
simply to point out some unfounded critical estimates
which have obtained currency among readers who have
but a partial acquaintance with Mr. Poe's more imaginative writings, and to record our own impressions of
the character and genius of the poet, as derived from
personal observation, and from the testimony of those
who knew him. Although he had been connected
with some of the leading magazines of the day, and
had edited for a time with great ability several success-
ful periodicals, Mr. Poe's literary reputation at the
North had been comparatively limited until his removal
to New York, in the autumn of 1847, when he became
personally known to a large circle of authors and
literary people, whose interest in his writings was
manifestly enhanced by the perplexing anomalies of his
character, and by the singular magnetism of his presence. One who knew him at this period of his life
says, "Everything about him distinguished him as a

man of mark ; his countenance, person, and gait, were alike characteristic. His features were regular, and decidedly handsome. His complexion was clear and dark ; the colour of his fine eyes seemingly a dark grey, but on closer inspection they were seen to be of that neutral, violet tint which is so difficult to define. His forehead was, without exception, the finest, in proportion and expression, that we have ever seen. The perceptive organs were not deficient, but seemed pressed out of the way by causality, comparison, and constructiveness. Close to these rose the proud arches of ideality. The coronal region was very imperfect, wanting in reverence and conscientiousness, and presenting a key to many of his literary characteristics. The ideas of right and wrong are as feeble in his chains of thought as in the literature of ancient Greece." We quote this description for its general fidelity. Its estimate of literary characteristics conveyed in the closing sentence we shall revert to in another place.

The engraved portraits of Mr. Poe have very little

2*

individuality; that prefixed to the volumes edited by
Dr. Griswold suggests, at first view, something of the
general contour of his face, but is utterly void of
character and expression; it has no sub-surface. The
original painting, now in possession of the New York
Historical Society, has the same cold, automatic look
that makes the engraving so valueless as a portrait to
those who remember the unmatched glory of his face
when roused from its habitually introverted and abstracted look by some favorite theme, or profound
emotion. Perhaps, from its peculiarly changeful and
translucent character, any adequate transmission of its
variable and subtle moods was impossible. By writers
personally unacquainted with Mr. Poe this engraving
has often been favourably noticed. Mr. Hannay, in a
Memoir prefixed to the first London edition of Poe's
Poems, calls it an interesting and characteristic portrait,
" a fine, thoughtful face with lineaments of delicacy,
such as belong only to genius or high blood—the
forehead grand and pale, the eye dark and gleaming

with sensibility and soul—a face to inspire men with interest and curiosity."

There is a quiet drawing-room in —— street, New York—a sort of fragrant and delicious "clover-nook" in the heart of the noisy city—where hung, some three years ago, the original painting from which this engraving is a copy. Happening to meet there at the time a company of authors and poets, among whom were Mary Forest, Alice and Phœbe Cary, the Stoddards, T. B. Aldrich, and others, we heard one of the party say, in speaking of the portrait, that its aspect was that of a beautiful and desolate shrine from which the Genius had departed, and that it recalled certain lines to one of the antique marbles :

"Oh melancholy eyes!
Oh empty eyes, from which the soul has gone
To see the far-off countries!"

Near this luminous but impassive face, with its sad and soulless eyes, was a portrait of Poe's unrelenting biographist. In a recess opposite hung a picture of the fascinating Mrs. ———, whose genius both had so fervently admired, and for whose coveted praise and friendship both had been competitors. Looking at the beautiful portrait of this lady—the face so full of enthusiasm, and dreamy, tropical sunshine—remembering the eloquent words of her praise, as expressed in the prodigal and passionate exaggerations of her verse, one ceases to wonder at the rivalries and enmities enkindled within the hearts of those who admired her genius and her grace—rivalries and enmities which the grave itself could not cancel or appease.

Of the portrait prefixed to the illustrated poems, recently published by Redfield, Mr. Willis says, "The reader who has the volume in his hand turns back musingly to look upon the features of the poet, in whom resided such inspiration. But, though well engraved and useful as recalling his features to those who knew them, with the angel shining through, the picture is from a daguerreotype, and gives no idea of the beauty of Edgar Poe. The exquisitely chiselled features, the habitual but intellectual melancholy, the clear pallor of the complexion, and the calm eye like the molten stillness of a slumbering volcano, composed a countenance of which this portrait is but the skeleton. After reading the Raven, Ulalume, Lenore, and Annabel Lee, the luxuriast in poetry will better conceive what his face might have been."

It was soon after his removal to New York that Mr. Poe became acquainted with the editors of the Mirror, and was employed by them as a writer for that Journal. Mr. Willis, in a recent notice of the illustrated poems, has paid an eloquent tribute to his memory, expressed in a spirit of rare kindliness and generosity.

From March 1845, to January 1846, he was associated with Mr. C. F. Briggs in editing the Broadway Journal. In the autumn of 1845 he was often seen at the brilliant literary circles in Waverley Place, where weekly reunions of noted artists and men of letters, at the house of an accomplished poetess, attracted some of the best intellectual society of the city. At the request of his hostess, Mr. Poe one evening electrified the gay company, assembled there, by the recitation of the wierd poem to whose sad, strange burden so many hearts have since echoed. This was a few weeks previous to the publication of the Raven in the American Review. Mrs. Browning, in a private letter, written a few weeks after its publication in England, says, "This vivid writing—this *power which is felt*—has produced a sensation here in England. Some of my friends are taken by the fear of it, and some by the music. I hear of persons who are haunted by the 'Nevermore,' and an acquaintance of mine who has the misfortune of possessing a bust of Pallas, cannot bear to look at it in the twilight. Then there is a tale going the rounds of the newspapers, about mesmerism, which is throwing us all into 'most admired disorder'—dreadful doubts as to whether it can be true, as the children say of ghost stories. The certain thing about it is the power of the writer."

A woman of fine genius, who at this time made his acquaintance, says, in some recently published comments on his writings : " It was in the brilliant circles that assembled in the winter of 1845-6 at the houses of Dr. Dewey, Miss Anna C. Lynch, Mr. Lawson, and others, that we first met Edgar Poe. His manners were at these re-unions refined and pleasing, and his style and scope of conversation that of a gentleman and a scholar. Whatever may have been his previous career, there was nothing in his appearance or manner to indicate his excesses. He delighted in the society of superior women, and had an exquisite perception of all graces of manner, and shades of expression. He was an admiring listener, and an unobtrusive observer. We all recollect the interest felt at the time in everything emanating from his pen—the relief it was from the dulness of ordinary writers—the certainty of something fresh and suggestive. His critiques were read with avidity; not that he convinced the judgment, but that people felt their ability and their courage. Right or wrong he was terribly in earnest." Like De Quincey, he never *supposed* anything, he always *knew*.

The peculiar character of his intellect seemed without a prototype in literature. He had more than De Quincey's power of analysis, with a constructive unity and completeness of which the great English essayist has given no indication. His pre-eminence in constructive and analytical skill was beginning to be universally admitted, and the fame and prestige of his genius were rapidly increasing. But the dangerous censorship he soon after assumed, as the author of a series of sketches, some of which have been since published as the "Literati," exposed him to frequent indignant criticism, while, by his personal errors and indiscretions, he drew upon himself much social censure and *espionage*, and became the victim of dishonoring accusations from which honor itself had forbidden him to exculpate himself.

It has been said, in allusion to the severity of his literary strictures, that a most fitting escutcheon for

Mr. Poe might have been found in the crest of Walter Scott's puissant Templar, Bois Guilbert,—a raven in full flight, holding in its claws a skull, and bearing the motto, " *Gare le Corbeau.*"

Mr. Longfellow has very generously said, in a letter to the editor of the Literary Messenger : " The harshness of his criticism I have always attributed to the irritation of a sensitive nature chafed by some indefinite sense of wrong."

A recent and not too lenient critic tells us that " it was his sensitiveness to artistic imperfections, rather than any malignity of feeling, that made his criticisms so severe, and procured him a host of enemies among persons towards whom he entertained no personal ill-will."

In evidence of the habitual courtesy and good-nature noticeable to all who best knew him in domestic and social life, we remember an incident that occurred at one of the soirées to which we have alluded. A lady, noted for her great lingual attainments, wishing

3

to apply a wholesome check to the vanity of a young
author, proposed inviting him to translate for the company a difficult passage in Greek, of which language
she knew him to be profoundly ignorant, although ͭ
given to a rather pretentious display of Greek quota-
tions in his published writings. Poe's earnest and
persistent remonstrance against this piece of *méchanceté*
alone averted the embarrassing test.

Sometimes his fair young wife was seen with him at
these weekly assemblages in Waverley Place. She sel-
dom took part in the conversation, but the memory of
her sweet and girlish face, always animated and viva-
cious, repels the assertion, afterwards so cruelly and
recklessly made, that she died a victim to the neglect
and unkindness of her husband, " who," as it has been
said, " deliberately sought her death that he might
embalm her memory in immortal dirges." An article
in Fraser's Magazine, published some two years ago,
repeats the assertion that Poe was the murderer of his
wife, " causing her to die of starvation and a broken

heart." Gilfillan, ascribing to him "passions controlled by the presence of art until they resembled sculptured flame," tells us that he caused the death of his wife that he might have a fitting theme for the Raven. A serious objection to this ingenious theory may perhaps be found in the "refractory fact" that the poem was published more than a year before the event which these persons assume it was intended to commemorate.

We might cite the testimony alike of friends and enemies to Poe's unvarying kindness towards his young wife and cousin, if other testimony were needed than that of the tender love still cherished for his memory by one whose life was made doubly desolate by his death—the sister of his father, and the mother of his Virginia.

It is well known to those acquainted with the parties that the young wife of Edgar Poe died of lingering consumption, which manifested itself even in her girl-hood. All who have had opportunities for observation in the matter have noticed her husband's tender devotion

to her during her prolonged illnesses. Even Dr. Griswold speaks of having visited him during a period of
illness caused by protracted anxiety and watching by
the side of his sick wife. It is true that notwithstanding
her vivacity and cheerfulness at the time we have
alluded to, her health was, even then, rapidly sinking;
and it was for her dear sake and for the recovery of
that peace which had been so fatally perilled amid the
irritations and anxieties of his New York life, that Poe
left the city and removed to the little Dutch cottage in
Fordham, where he passed the three remaining years of
his life. It was to this quiet haven in the beautiful
spring of 1846, when the fruit trees were all in bloom
and the grass in its freshest verdure, that he brought
his Virginia to die. Here he watched her failing
breath in loneliness and privation through many solitary
moons, until, on a desolate, dreary day of the ensuing
winter, he saw her remains borne from beneath its lowly
roof to a neighbouring cemetery. It was towards the
close of the year following her death—his "most

immemorial year "—that he wrote the strange threnody
of "Ulalume." This poem, perhaps the most original
and wierdly suggestive of all his poems, resembles at
first sight some of Turner's landscapes, being apparently
"without form and void, and having darkness on the
face of it." It is, nevertheless, in its basis, although not
in the precise correspondence of time, simply historical.
Such was the poet's lonely midnight walk—such, amid
the desolate memories and sceneries of the hour, was
the new-born hope enkindled within his heart at sight
of the morning star—

"Astarte's bediamonded crescent"—

coming up as the beautiful harbinger of love and
happiness yet awaiting him in the untried future, and
such the sudden transition of feeling, the boding dread,
that supervened on discovering that which had at first
been unnoted, that it shone, as if in mockery or in
warning, directly over the sepulchre of the lost "Ulalume." A writer in the London Critic, after quoting

3*

the opening stanzas of Ulalume, says, "These to many
will appear only *words*, but what wondrous words!
What a spell they wield! What a withered unity there
is in them! The instant they are uttered a misty
picture with a tarn, dark as a murderer's eye, below,
and the thin yellow leaves of October fluttering above,
exponents of a misery which scorns the name of sorrow,
is hung up in the chambers of your soul for ever."

An English writer, now living in Paris, the author
of some valuable contributions to our American periodicals, passed several weeks at the little cottage in Fordham, in the early autumn of 1847, and described to us,
with a truly English appreciativeness, its unrivalled
neatness and the quaint simplicity of its interior and
surroundings. It was at the time bordered by a flower-
garden, whose clumps of rare dahlias and brilliant beds
of fall flowers showed, in the careful culture bestowed
upon them, the fine floral taste of the inmates.

An American writer, who visited the cottage during
the summer of the same year, described it as half

buried in fruit trees, and as having a thick grove of pines in its immediate neighbourhood. The proximity of the railroad, and the increasing population of the little village, have since wrought great changes in the place. Round an old cherry-tree, near the door, was a broad bank of greenest turf. The neighbouring beds of mignonette and heliotrope, and the pleasant shade above, made this a favourite seat. Rising at four o'clock in the morning, for a walk to the magnificent Aqueduct bridge over Harlem river, our informant found the poet, with his mother, standing on the turf beneath the cherry-tree, eagerly watching the movements of two beautiful birds that seemed contemplating a settlement in its branches. He had some rare tropical birds in cages, which he cherished and petted with assiduous care. Our English friend described him as giving to his birds and his flowers a delighted attention that seemed quite inconsistent with the gloomy and grotesque character of his writings. A favourite cat, too, enjoyed his friendly patronage, and often when he was engaged in composition it seated itself on his shoulder, purring as in complacent approval of the work proceeding under its supervision.

During Mr. Poe's residence at Fordham a walk to High Bridge was one of his favourite and habitual recreations. The water of the Aqueduct is conveyed across the river on a range of lofty granite arches, which rise to the height of a hundred and forty-five feet above high-water level. On the top a turfed and grassy road, used only by foot-passengers, and flanked on either side by a low parapet of granite, makes one of the finest promenades imaginable.

The winding river and the high rocky shores at the western extremity of the bridge are seen to great advantage from this lofty avenue. In the last melancholy years of his life—"the lonesome latter years"—Poe was accustomed to walk there at all times of the day and night; often pacing the then solitary pathway for hours without meeting a human being. A little to the east of the cottage rises a ledge of rocky

ground, partly covered with pines and cedars, command-
ing a fine view of the surrounding country and of the
picturesque college of St. John's, which had at that time
in its neighbourhood an avenue of venerable old trees.
This rocky ledge was also one of the poet's favourite
resorts. Here through long summer days and through
solitary, star-lit nights he loved to sit, dreaming his gorgeous waking dreams, or pondering the deep problems
of "The Universe,"—that grand " prose-poem" to which
he devoted the last and maturest energies of his wonderful intellect. The abstracted enthusiasm with which
he pursued his great quest into the cosmogony of the
universe is an earnest of the passionate intellectual sincerity which we shall presently take occasion to illustrate.

Wanting in that supreme central force or faculty of
the mind, whose function is a God-conscious and God-
adoring faith, Edgar Poe sought earnestly and conscien-
tiously for such solution of the great problems of
thought as were alone attainable to an intellect hurled

from its balance by the abnormal preponderance of the analytical and imaginative faculties. It was to this very disproportion that we are indebted for some of those marvellous intellectual creations, which, as we shall hope to prove, had an important significance and an especial adaptation to the time.

A very intolerant article on Mr. Poe has recently been republished in this country from the Edinburgh Review for April 1858, in which the most injurious anecdotes of Dr. Griswold's memoir have been patiently copied and italicised, and their enormities enhanced by the gratuitous suppositions and assumptions of the writer.

As an instance of the inconsequent reasoning in which the reviewer sometimes indulges, we quote a single passage from the article in question. "It is," says the Edinburgh critic, "a curious example of Poe's superficial acquaintance with the literature of other lands, that in recapitulating the titles of a mysterious library of books in 'the House of Usher' he quotes among a list of cabalistical volumes Gresset's 'Vertvert,' *evidently in complete ignorance of what he is talking about. Gresset's 'Vertvert' is the antipodes of Poe's 'Raven,'* though the comic interest of the former and the tragic interest of the latter turn alike on the reiteration of bird-language."

The process of reasoning by which Mr. Poe's "superficial acquaintance with the literature of other lands" is deducible from the fact that "Gresset's 'Vertvert' is the antipodes of Poe's 'Raven,'" may be very apparent to the learned reviewer, but is certainly not quite clear to the common reader.

We are not aware that any of the works cited in this catalogue bear a resemblance to the Raven. Mr. Poe must certainly be acquitted of intending to suggest such a resemblance, since the Raven was at the time unwritten. The Edinburgh critic, after admitting that Poe's Raven belongs to "that rare and remarkable class of productions that suffice, *singly*, to make a reputation," assumes, oddly enough, that "the originality apparent

in Mr. Poe's writings is due rather to the deformity of
his moral character than to the vigor or freshness of
his intellect," and, finding himself "profoundly im-
pressed by Poe's wonderful solutions of the most difficult problems," suspects that "it is after all, an easy
thing for man to solve the riddles which he himself has
fabricated."

There is a prevalent impression among critics and
readers who have never felt the magnetism of Poe's
wierd imagination, nor come into full rapport with his
genius, that his intellectual creations were always the
result of deliberate effort and artistic skill; that they
were not genuine outgrowths of the inward life but
arbitrary creations of the will and the intellect.

This opinion, founded in part upon the subtlety and
refinement of his analytical faculty, has been seemingly
guaranteed by some of his own statements in regard to
his methods of composition.   A writer in the "North
American" characterizes his poetry as "word-maneu-
vering," and one of his critics, sitting at the time in

Harper's "Easy-chair," says, "Such curious and beautiful performances as Poe's 'Raven' and 'Sleigh-bells' are not poems; they are, simply, ingenious experiments upon the sound of words." Were this grand lyric of "The Bells" simply a lyric of "Sleigh-bells" as the "Easy-chair" pleasantly calls it, when were Sleigh-bells ever heard to ring so merrily before? Listen!

> "How they tinkle, tinkle, tinkle
> In the icy air of night!
> While the stars that oversprinkle
> All the heavens seem to twinkle
> With a crystalline delight;
> Keeping time, time, time,
> In a sort of Runic rhyme,
> To the tintinnabulation that so musically wells
> From the bells, bells, bells, bells,
> Bells, bells, bells—
> From the jingling and the tinkling of the bells."

It cannot indeed be denied that the mere artistic treatment of this poem is truly marvellous. The metallic

4

ring and resonance—the vibration and reverberation of the rhythm—is such that one of its admirers says, "We can never read it without pausing after every verse to let the *peals of sound* die away on the 'bosom of the palpitating air,' that we may commence the succeeding stanza in silence." Another, who appreciates its ideal truth of conception not less than its high rhythmical art, says, "I was astonished one night in watching a conflagration, and repeating, amid the clash and clang of the alarm-bells, the third stanza of the poem, to find how marvellously the movement of the verse *timed* with the peals of sound, and how truly the poem reproduced the sense-of danger which the sound of the bells, and the glare and mad ascension of the flames, and the pallor of the moonlight conveyed. All the poetry of a conflagration is in that stanza, both in sound and sense, and Dante himself could not have rendered it more truly."

So many faculties were brought into play in the expression of Poe's poetical compositions that readers in whom the critical intellect prevails over the imaginative often acknowledge the refined art, the tact, the subtlety, the faultless method, while the potent *magnetism* of his genius utterly escapes them. There are persons whom nature has made non-conductors to this sort of electricity.

The critic of the "North American" to whose strictures we have alluded, charges him with overlooking moral and spiritual ideas, and calls his works "rich and elaborate pieces of art," wanting in "the *vis vitea* which alone can make of words living things." Bayne, on the other hand, in his fine essay on "Tennyson and his Teachers," alludes to the "Haunted Palace" of "the great American poet," and contrasts its wonderfully spiritual, subjective, and ideal character with the rich and accurate detail of Tennyson's "Palace of Art." He classes the American poet with those who have scattered *imaginative spells* rather than finished elaborate imaginative pictures. A greater mistake in literary criticism could not well be made than that which is evinced in the frequent application of the word "sensu-

ous" to the singularly ideal and subjective character of
Poe's imaginative creations. We do not of course
intend to include among these, his stories of a purely
inventive or grotesque character.

It is not to be questioned that Poe was a consummate
master of language—that he had sounded all the secrets
of rhythm—that he understood and availed himself of
all its resources; the balance and poise of syllables—
the alternations of emphasis and cadence—of vowel-
sounds and consonants—and all the metrical sweetness
of "phrase and metaphrase." Yet this consummate art
was in him united with a rare simplicity. He was the
most genuine of enthusiasts, as we think we shall presently show. His genius would follow no leadings
but those of his own imperial intellect. With all his
vast mental resources he could never write an occasional
poem, or adapt himself to the taste of a popular audi-
ence. His graver narratives and fantasies are often
related with an earnest simplicity, solemnity, and apparent fidelity, attributable, not so much to a deliberate

artistic purpose, as to that power of vivid and intense conception that made his dreams realities, and his life a dream.

The strange fascination—the unmatched charm of his conversation—consisted in its *genuineness*. Even Dr. Griswold, who has studiously represented him as cold, passionless, and perfidious, admits that his conversation was at times almost "supra-mortal in its eloquence;" that "his large and variably expressive eyes looked repose or shot fiery tumult into theirs who listened, while his own face glowed, or was changeless in pallor, as his imagination quickened his blood or drew it back frozen to his heart."

These traits are not the possible accompaniments of attributes which Dr. Griswold has elsewhere ascribed to him. As a conversationist we do not remember his equal. We have heard the veteran Landor (called by high authority the best talker in England) discuss with scathing sarcasm the popular writers of the day, convey his political animosities by fierce invectives on the "pretentious coxcomb, Albert," and "the cunning knave, Napoleon," or describe, in words of strange depth and tenderness, the peerless charm of goodness and the naive social graces in the beautiful mistress of Gore House, "the most gorgeous Lady Blessington." We have heard the Howadji talk of the gardens of Damascus till the air seemed purpled and perfumed with its roses. We have listened to the trenchant and vivid talk of the Autocrat; to the brilliant and exhaustless colloquial resources of John Neal, and Margaret Fuller. We have heard the racy talk of Orestes Brownson in the old days of his freedom and power, have listened to the serene wisdom of Alcott, and treasured up memorable sentences from the golden lips of Emerson. Unlike the conversational power evinced by any of these was the earnest, opulent, unpremeditated speech of Edgar Poe.

Like his writings it presented a combination of qualities rarely met with in the same person; a cool, decisive judgment, a wholly unconventional courtesy and sincere grace of manner, and an imperious enthusiasm which brought all hearers within the circle of its influence.

J. M. Daniel, Esq., United States Minister at Turin, who knew Poe well during the last years of his life, says of him, "His conversation was the very best we have ever listened to. We have never heard any so suggestive of thought, or any from which one gained so much. On literary subjects it was the essence of correct and profound criticism divested of all formal pedantries and introductory ideas—the kernel clear of the shell. He was not a brilliant talker in the common, after-dinner sense of the word; he was not a maker of fine points, or a frequent sayer of funny things. What he said was prompted entirely by the moment, and seemed uttered for the pleasure of uttering it. In his animated moods he talked with an abstracted earnestness as if he were dictating to an amanuensis, and, if he spoke of individuals, his ideas ran upon their moral and intellectual qualities rather than upon the idiosyncrasies of their active visible phenomena, or the peculiarities of their manner."

We have said that the charm of his conversation consisted in its genuineness—its wonderful directness and sincerity. We believe, too, that in the artistic utterance of poetic emotion he was at all times passionately genuine. His proud reserve, his profound melancholy, his unworldliness—may we not say his *unearthliness* of nature—made his character one very difficult of comprehension to the casual observer. The complexity of his intellect, its incalculable resources, and his masterly control of those resources when brought into requisition for the illustration of some favorite theme, or cherished creation, led to the current belief that its action was purely arbitrary—that he could write without emotion or earnestness at the deliberate dictation of the will. A certain class of his writings undeniably exhibits the faculties of ingenuity and invention in a prominent and distinctive light. But it must not be forgotten that there was another phase of his mind— one not less distinctive and characteristic of his genius— which manifested itself in creations of a totally different order and expression. ˈ It can hardly have escaped the notice of the most careless reader that certain ideas exercised over him the power of fascination. They return, again and again, in his stories and poems and seem like the utterances of a mind possessed with thoughts, emotions, and images of which the will and the understanding take little cognizance. In the delineation of these, his language often acquires a power and pregnancy eluding all attempts at analysis. It is then that by a few miraculous words he evokes emotional states or commands pictorial effects which live for ever in the memory and from a part of its eternal inheritance. No analysis can dissect—no criticism can disenchant them.

As specimens of the class we have indicated read "Ligeia," "Morella," "Eleanora." Observe in them the prevailing and dominant thoughts of his inner life—ideas of "fate and metaphysical aid"—of psychal and spiritual agencies, energies and potences. See in them intimations of mysterious phenomena

which, at the time when these fantasies were indited,
were regarded as fables and dreams, but which have
since (in their phenomenal aspect simply) been recognised as matters of popular experience and scientific
research.

In "Ligeia," the sad and stately symmetry of the sentences, their rhythmical cadence, the Moresque sumptu-
ousness of imagery with which the story is invested, and
the wierd metempsychosis which it records, produce an
effect on the reader altogether peculiar in character
and, as we think, quite inexplicable without a reference
to the supernatural inspiration which seems to pervade
them. |In the moods of mind and phases of passion
which this story represents we have no laboured artistic
effects | we look into the haunted chambers of the
poet's own mind and see, as through a veil, the strange
experiences of his inner life; while, in the dusk magnifi-
cence of its imagery, we have the true heraldic blazonry
of an imagination royally dowered and descended.   In
this, as in all that class of stories we have named, the

author's mind seems struggling desperately and vainly with the awful mystery of Death.

In "Morella," as in "Ligeia," the parties are occupied with the same mystic philosophies—engrossed in the same recondite questions of " life and death and spiritual unity," questions of "that identity which, at death, is, or is not, lost forever." Each commemorates a psychal attraction which transcends the dissolution of the mortal body and oversweeps the grave; the passionate soul of the departed transfusing itself through the organism of another to manifest its deathless love. Who does not remember as a strain of Æonian melody the story of "Eleanora ? " Who does not lapse into a dream as he remembers the "River of Silence" and " The Valley of the many-colored Grass ?"

In this story the purport, though less apparent to the general reader, and differently interpreted by a writer in the "North American Review," is still the same as in the preceding. Read the closing sentences, so eloquent with a tender and mysterious meaning, which record,

after the death of the beloved Eleanora, the appearance
"from a far, far distant and unknown land" of the
Seraph Ermengarde. Observe, too, in these closing
lines the indication, so often manifest in Poe's poems
and stories, of a lingering pity and sorrow for the dead;
—an ever-recurring pang of remorse in the fear of
having grieved them by some involuntary wrong of
desertion or forgetfulness.

This haunting remembrance—this sad, remorseful pity
for the departed, is everywhere a distinguishing feature
in his prose and poetry.

The existence of such a feeling as a prevalent mood
of his mind, of which we have abundant evidence, is
altogether incompatible with that cold sensualism with
which he has been so ignorantly charged. So far from
being selfish or heartless his devotional fidelity to the
memory of those he loved would by the world be
regarded as fanatical. A characteristic incident of his
boyhood will illustrate the passionate fidelity which we
have ascribed to him. While at the academy in

Richmond, which he entered in his twelfth year, he one day accompanied a schoolmate to his home, where he saw for the first time Mrs. H———— S————, the mother of his young friend. This lady, on entering the room, took his hand and spoke some gentle and gracious words of welcome, which so penetrated the sensitive heart of the orphan boy as to deprive him of the power of speech, and, for a time, almost of consciousness itself. He returned home in a dream, with but one thought, one hope in life—to hear again the sweet and gracious words that had made the desolate world so beautiful to him, and filled his lonely heart with the oppression of a new joy. This lady afterwards became the confidant of all his boyish sorrows, and her's was the one redeeming influence that saved and guided him in the earlier days of his turbulent and passionate youth. After the visitation of strange and peculiar sorrows she died, and for months after her decease it was his habit to visit nightly the cemetery where the object of his boyish idolatry lay entombed. The thought of her—

sleeping there in her loneliness—filled his heart with a profound, incommunicable sorrow. When the nights were very dreary and cold, when the autumnal rains fell and the winds wailed mournfully over the graves, he lingered longest and came away most regretfully.

It was the image of this lady, long and tenderly, and sorrowfully cherished, that suggested the stanzas "to Helen," published among the poems written in his youth, which Russell Lowell says have in them a grace and symmetry of outline such as few poets ever attain, and which are valuable as displaying "what can only be expressed by the contradictory phrase of *innate experience.*"

As the lines do not appear in the latest editions of his poems we give them here.

> "Helen, thy beauty is to me
>   Like those Nicean barks of yore,
> That gently, o'er a perfumed sea,
>   The weary, wayworn wanderer bore
>   To his own native shore.

On desperate seas long wont to roam,
  Thy hyacinth hair, thy classic face,
Thy Naiad airs have brought me home
  To the glory that was Greece,
To the grandeur that was Rome.

Lo! in yon brilliant window niche,
  How statue-like I see thee stand,
The agate lamp within thy hand!
Ah, Psyche, from the regions which
  Are Holy Land!" .

In a letter now before us, written within a twelve-month of his death, Edgar Poe speaks of the love which inspired these verses as "the one, idolatrous, and purely *ideal* love" of his passionate boyhood.

In one of the numbers of Russell's Magazine there is a transcript of the first published version of the exquisite poem entitled "Lenore," commencing

"Ah broken is the golden bowl! the spirit flown forever,
  Let the bell toll! a saintly soul floats on the Stygian river."

It is remarkable that, in this earlier version, instead of
LENORE we have the name of HELEN. The lines were
afterwards greatly altered and improved in structure
and expression, and the name of Lenore was introduced,
apparently for its adaptation to rhythmical effect. Whatever may be the meaning that underlies this strange
funeral anthem it will always be admired for the trium-
phant music of its sorrow and for its sombre pomp of
words. We may trust that the "Sabbath Song" did
indeed

"Go up to God so solemnly the dead could feel no wrong."

The ideas which haunted the brain of the young poet
during his watch in the lonely church-yard—the shape-
less fears and phantasms,

"Flapping from out their Condor wings
Invisible Woe!"

were the same which overwhelmed De Quincey at the
burial of his sweet sister and playmate, as described by
him in the "Suspiria De Profundis"—ideas of terror

and indescribable awe at the thought of that mysterious waking sleep, that powerless and dim vitality, in which "the dead" are presumed, according to our popular theology, to await " the general resurrection at the last day." What wonder that the phantoms of "Shadow" and "Silence," once evoked there, could never be exorcised! What wonder that "the fable which the Demon told in the shadow of the tomb" haunted him for ever!

"Now there are strange tales in the volumes of the Magi—in the iron-bound, melancholy volumes of the Magi—glorious histories of the Heaven, and of the Earth, and of the mighty Sea—and of the Genii that overruled the sea and the earth and the lofty heaven; there was much lore, too, in the sayings of the Sybils. and holy, holy things were heard of old by the dim leaves that trembled around Dodona—but, *as Allah liveth, that fable which the Demon told me as he sat by my side in the shadow of the tomb, I hold to be the most wonderful of all! And as the Demon made an end of his story, he fell back within the cavity of the tomb and laughed. And I could not laugh with the Demon, and he cursed me because I could not laugh.* And the lynx which dwelleth forever in the tomb, came out and sat at the feet of the Demon and looked him steadily in the face."

These solitary church-yard vigils, with all their associated memories, present a key to much that seems strange and abnormal in the poet's after life. Questions which no human tongue could answer, no human knowledge satisfy or silence, then found an utterance in the vast and desolate chambers of his imagination, and their mournful echoes are heard again and again in the magic cadences of his verse. In the "Colloquy of Monos and Una" he has imagined all the phases of sentient life in the grave, and in the "Bridal Ballad" are stanzas which, as read by the author, were full of a wild, sad pathos not easily forgotten. We will instance only two of the stanzas although their rhythmical effect is injured by their separation from those which precede and accompany them.

"And my lord he loves me well;
  But when first he breathed his vow
The words rang as a knell,
And the voice seemed *his* who fell
In the battle down the dell,
  And who is happy now.

*   *   *   *   *

Would God I could awaken!
  For I dream I know not how,
And my soul is sorely shaken
Lest an evil step be taken—
Lest the dead, who is forsaken,
  May not be happy now."

The thought which informs so many of his tales and poems betrays its sad sincerity even in his critical writings, as, for instance, in a notice of " Undine" in the " Marginalia." Yet it has been said of him that "he had no touch of human feeling or of human pity," that "he loved no one but himself"—that "he was an abnormal and monstrous creation,"—" possessed by legions of devils." The most injurious epithets have been heaped upon his name and the most improbable and calumnious stories recorded as veritable histories. Ten years have passed since his death, and while the popular interest in his writings and the popular estimate of his genius increases from year to year, these acknowledged calumnies are still going the round of the foreign periodicals and are still being republished at home.

We believe that with the exception of Mr. Willis's generous tributes to his memory, some candid and friendly articles by the Editor of the Literary Messenger, and an eloquent and vigorous article in Russell's Magazine by Mr. J. Wood Davidson, of Columbia, S.C. (who has appreciated his genius and his sorrow more justly perhaps, than any of his American critics) this great and acknowledged wrong to the dead has been permitted to pass without public rebuke or protest.

In the memoir prefixed to the Illustrated Poems, it is said of him that "his religion was a worship of the beautiful," which is emphatically true, and that "he knew no beauty but that which is purely sensuous," which is, as emphatically, untrue. We appeal from this last assertion to Mr. Poe's own exposition of his poetic theory. He recognises the elements of poetic emotion—the emotion of the beautiful—"*in all noble thoughts, in all holy impulses, in all chivalrous, generous, and self-sacrificing deeds.*" His "æsthetic religion," which has been so strangely misapprehended was simply a recognition of the divine and inseparable harmonies of the supremely Beautiful and the supremely Good.

The author of the very able and systematic critique in the North American Review (which is, nevertheless, essentially false in all its estimates of intellectual and moral character) tells us that he "*repudiated moral uses* in his prose fictions as in his poetry, and that if moral or spiritual truths are found in them they must have got there accidentally, without the author's permission or knowledge." This is very unjust. To prove its injustice we have only once more to quote the author's own words. "*Taste,*" the sense of the beautiful, "*holds intimate relations with the intellect and the moral sense ;*"

from the moral sense it is separated by so faint a
difference that Aristotle has not hesitated to place some
of its operations among the virtues themselves." Again,
"The poetic sense is strictly and simply the human
aspiration for supernal beauty. It is no mere apprecia-
tion of the beauty before us, but a wild effort to reach
the beauty above—a prescience of that loveliness whose
very elements, perhaps, appertain to Eternity alone."

The current strictures on Poe's sinful worship of
Beauty remind us of the satirist, Shoppe, in Jean Paul's
"Titan," who says, "In one respect we Germans are far
in advance of the Greeks and Italians. We never seek
the Beautiful without looking for collateral advantages;
our caryatides must uphold pulpits, and our angels bear
baptismal fonts."

We are ready to admit, with the severe critic of the
North American, that a very large proportion of Poe's
stories are filled with monstrous and appalling images—
that many of them oppress the reader like frightful
incubi, from whose influence he vainly tries to escape.

Ruskin tells us, in his treatise on the Grotesque, that it is the trembling of the human soul in the presence of Death which most of all disturbs the images on the intellectual mirror, investing them with the grotesque ghastliness of fitful dreams. "If the mind be not healthful and serene the wider the scope of its glance and the grander the truths of which it obtains an insight the more fantastic and fearful are these distorted images."

Yet, as out of mighty and terrific discords noblest harmonies are sometimes evolved, so through the purgatorial ministries of awe and terror, and through the haunting Nemesis of doubt, Poe's restless and unappeased soul was urged on to the fulfilment of its appointed work—groping out blindly towards the light, and marking the approach of great spiritual truths by the very depth of the shadow it projected against them.

It would seem that the true point of view from which his genius should be regarded has yet to be sought.

We are not of those who believe that any order of
genius is revealed to us in vain ; nor do we believe that
the age would have gained anything if the author of the
Raven had proved another Wordsworth, or another
Longfellow. These far-wandering comets, not less than
"the regular, calm stars," obey a law and follow a
pathway that has been marked out for them by infinite
Wisdom and essential Love. That the genius of Poe
had its peculiar mission and significance in relation to
the age we cannot doubt. Every man of electric temperament and prophetic genius represents, or rather
anticipates, with more or less of consciousness and direct
volition, those latent ideas which are about to unfold
themselves in humanity. It is thus that Müller accounts
for the origin of the Greek Mythus, the simple invention
of which he pronounces to be impossible, if by *invention*
is meant a free and deliberate treatment of something
known to be untrue. He regards the originators of the
Greek Mythus merely as the more passive recipients and
skilful exponents who first gave form and expression to

those spiritual ideas which were tending to organic development at that particular stage of the world's progress—"the foci in which the scattered rays of spiritual consciousness were concentrating themselves to be radiated forth with new intensity." When Poe's genius began to unfold itself the age was moving feverously and restlessly through processes of transition and development which seemed about to unsettle all things, yet, gave no clear indication of whither they were leading us.

In our own country, Mr. Emerson's assertion of the transcendental side of the ever-recurring question between idealism and materialism marked the reaction of intellectual and spiritual tendencies against the materialism and literalism of the churches. Through him the fine idealism of the German Mystics penetrated our literature and spiritualized our philosophies. His novel statements of truth had in them a strange force and directness, startling the sleepers like the naive cadences of a child's voice heard amid the falsetto tones

6

of the conventicle or the theatre. What a sovran
grace of sincerity in his chapter on Experience. What
noble ethics in his statement of spiritual laws. Yet, if
we turn to the pages of Emerson and look for the
evidences of his belief in the soul's individual immortality, we shall find that the words he has uttered on the
subject express, for the most part, either a purely
Oriental indifference or an aimless and anxious ques-
tioning. In his lecture to the Divinity Students of
Cambridge, protesting against the formalism and famine
of the churches, he told them that the faith of the
Puritans was dying out and none arising in its stead—
that the eye of youth was not lighted by the hope of
other worlds—that literature had become frivolous and
science cold. In his lecture on "The Times" he says,
"We drift like white sail across the wide·ocean, now
bright on the wave, now darkling in the trough of the
sea;—but from what port did we sail? Who knows?
Or to what port are we bound? Who knows? There
is no one to tell us but such poor weather-tossed

mariners as ourselves, whom we speak as we pass, or who have hoisted some signal from afar, or floated to us some letter in a bottle. But what know they more than we?" In another of his essays he says, "I cannot tell if these wonderful qualities which now house together in this mortal frame shall ever reassemble in equal activity in a similar frame, but this one thing I know, that the *law* which clothes us with humanity remains new. We are immortal with the immortality of this law."

These expressions indicate the pervading scepticism of the time. Coming, as they do, from a man who had been educated as a clergyman—a man for whose large culture and liberal faith in humanity the pulpits of the existing church seemed to offer no sufficient platform— they have an emphasis which no added word could heighten.

The negation of Carlyle, and the boundless affirmation of Emerson, served but to stimulate without satisfying the intellect. The liberal ethics of Fourier, with his

elaborate social economies and systems of petrified
harmony, were leading his disciples through forlorn
enterprises to hopeless failures. A "divine dissatisfaction" was everywhere apparent. De Quincey saw
something fearful and portentous in the vast accessions
to man's physical resources that marked the time,
unaccompanied by any improvement in psychal and
spiritual knowledge. Goethe had made his great dra-
matic poem an expression of the soul's craving for a
knowledge of spiritual existences—

> "O giebt es geister in der luft
>
> Die zwischen Erd' und Himmel weben,
>
> So steiget nieder aus den golden duft,
>
> Und furht mich weg zu neuem bunten leben."

Wordsworth, in his finest imaginative poem, "Laoda-
mia," represents and half reproves this longing. Byron
iterates it with a proud and passionate vehemence in
"Manfred." Shelley's sad heart of unbelief, finding
refuge in a despair too deep for aspiration, stands

apart, as Elizabeth Browning has so finely sculptured him,

————" In his white ideal
All statue-blind,"

while Keats lies sleeping, like his own "Endymion," lost in dreams of the "dead Past." Then, sadder, and lonelier, and more unbelieving than any of these, Edgar Poe came to sound the very depths of the abyss. The unrest and faithlessness of the age culminated in him. Nothing so solitary, nothing so hopeless, nothing so desolate as his spirit in its darker moods has been instanced in the literary history of the nineteenth century.

It has been said that his theory, as expressed in "Eureka," of the universal diffusion of Deity in and through all things, is identical with the Brahminical faith as expressed in the Bagvat Gita. But those who will patiently follow the vast reaches of his thought in this sublime poem of the "Universe" will find that he

arrives at a form of unbelief far more appalling than
that expressed in the gloomy Pantheism of India, since
it assumes that the central, creative Soul is, alternately,
not *diffused* only, but merged and *lost* in the universe,
and the universe in it: "A new universe swelling into
existence or subsiding into nothingness at every throb
of the Heart Divine." The creative Energy, therefore,
"*now* exists solely in the diffused matter and spirit, of
the existing universe." The author assumes, moreover,
that each individual soul retains in its youth a dim
consciousness of vast dooms and destinies far distant in
the bygone time, and infinitely awful; from which
inherent consciousness the conventional "World-Rea-
son" at last awakens it as from a dream. "It says
you live, and the time was when you lived not. You
have been created. An Intelligence exists greater than
your own, and it is only through this Intelligence that
you live at all." "These things," he says, "*we struggle
to comprehend and cannot:* cannot, because being untrue,
they are of necessity incomprehensible.

"No thinking man lives who, at some luminous point of his life, has not felt himself lost amid the surges of futile efforts at understanding or believing that anything exists *greater than his own soul*. The intense, overwhelming dissatisfaction and rebellion at the thought, together with the omniprevalent aspirations at perfection are but the spiritual, coincident with the material, struggles towards the original Unity. The material *and* spiritual God *now* exists solely in the diffused matter and Spirit of the Universe, and the regathering of this diffused Matter and Spirit will be but the reconstitution of the *purely* Spiritual and Individual God."

In a copy of the original edition of Eureka, purchased at the recent sale of Dr Griswold's library, the following note was found inscribed in the handwriting of the author on the half blank page at the end of the volume. It is singularly ingenious and characteristic.

"*Note.*—The pain of the consideration that we shall lose our individual identity, ceases at once when we further reflect that the process, as above described, is neither more nor less than that of the absorption by each individual intelligence, of all other intelligences (that is of the Universe) into its own. That God may be all in all, *each* must become God."

This proud self-assertion betrays a mysterious isolation from the "Heart Divine" which fills us with sadness and awe.

We confess to a half faith in the old superstition of the significance of anagrams when we find, in the transposed letters of Edgar Poe's name, the words *a God-peer;* words which, taken in connexion with his daring speculations, seem to have in them a mocking and malign import "which is not man's nor angel's."

Yet, while the author of Eureka, like Lucretius,

> ———" dropped his plummet down the broad,
> Deep Universe and found no God,"

his works are, as if unconsciously, filled with an overwhelming sense of the power and majesty of Deity;

they are even dark with reverential awe. His proud intellectual assumption of the supremacy of the individual soul *was but an expression of its imperious longings for immortality and its recoil from the haunting phantasms of death and annihilation ;* while the theme of all his more imaginative writings is, as we have said, a love that survives the dissolution of the mortal body and oversweeps the grave. His mental and temperamental idiosyncrasies fitted him to come readily into rapport with psychal and spiritual influences. Many of his strange narratives had a degree of truth in them which he was unwilling to avow. In one of this class he makes the narrator say, "I cannot even now regard these experiences as a dream, yet it is difficult to say how otherwise they should be termed. *Let us suppose only that the soul of man, to-day, is on the brink of stupendous psychal discoveries.*"

Dante tells us that

———"minds dreaming near the dawn
Are of the truth presageful."

Edgar Poe's dreams were assuredly often presageful and significant, and while he but dimly apprehended through the higher reason the truths which they foreshadowed, he riveted public attention upon them by the strange fascination of his style, the fine analytical temper of his intellect, and, above all, by the wierd splendors of his imagination, compelling men to read and to accredit as *possible truths* his most marvellous conceptions.   He often spoke of the imageries and incidents of his inner life as more vivid and veritable than those of his outer experience.   We find in some pencilled notes appended to a manuscript copy of one of his later poems the words, " All that I have here expressed was actually present to me.   Remember the mental condition which gave rise to 'Ligeia'—recall the passage of which I spoke, and observe the coincidence."   With all the fine alchymy of his subtle intellect he sought to analyze the character and conditions of this introverted life.   " I regard these visions," he says, "even as they arise, with an awe which in some measure moderates or tranquillizes the ecstacy—I so regard them through a conviction that this ecstacy, in itself, is of a character supernal to the human nature—*is a glimpse of the spirit's outer world.*" He had that constitutional determination to reverie which, according to De Quincey, alone enables a man to dream magnificently, and which, as we have said, made his dreams realities and his life a dream. His mind was indeed a "Haunted Palace," echoing to the footfalls of angels and demons. "No man," he says, "has recorded, no man has dared to record, the wonders of his inner life."

Is there, then, no significance in this "supernatural soliciting?" Is there no evidence of a wise purpose, an epochal fitness, in the appearance, at this precise era, of a mind so rarely gifted, and accessible from peculiarities of psychal and physical organization to the subtle vibrations of an ethereal medium conveying but feeble impressions to the senses of ordinary persons; a mind which, "following darkness like a dream," wandered for ever with insatiate curiosity on the confines of that

—" wild, wierd clime, that lieth sublime

Out of Space, out of Time !

By each spot the most unholy,

In each nook most melancholy,"

seeking to solve the problem of that phantasmal Shadow-Land, which, through a class of phenomena unprece-dented in the world's history, was about to attest itself as an actual plane of conscious and progressive life, the mode and measure of whose relations with our own are already recognised as legitimate objects of scientific research by the most candid and competent thinkers of our time ?   We assume that, in the abnormal manifes-tations of a genius so imperative and so controlling, this epochal significance *is* most strikingly apparent.   Jean Paul says truly that " there is more poetic fitness, more method, a more intelligible purpose in the biographies which God Almighty writes than in all the inventions of poets and novelists."

The peculiarities of Edgar Poe's organization and temperament doubtless exposed him to peculiar infirmities. We need not discuss them here. They have been already too elaborately and painfully illustrated elsewhere to need further comment. How fearfully he expiated them only those who best knew and loved him can ever know. We are told that ideas of right and wrong are wholly ignored by him—that " no recognitions of conscience or remorse are to be found on his pages." If not *there* where, then, shall we look for them ? In William Wilson, in " The Man of the Crowd," and in " The Tell-Tale Heart," the retributions of conscience are portrayed with a terrible fidelity. In yet another of his stories, which we will not name, the fearful fatality of crime—the dreadful fascination consequent on the indulgence of a perverse will is portrayed with a relentless and awful reality. May none ever read it who do not need the fearful lesson which it brands on the memory in characters of fire ! In the relation of this remarkable story we recognise the power of a genius like that which sustains us in traversing the lowest depths of Dante's "Inferno." The rapid descent

7

in crime which it delineates, and which becomes at last
involuntary, reminds us of the subterranean staircase by
which Vathek and Nouronihar reached the Hall of
Eblis, where, as they descended, they felt their steps
frightfully accelerated till they seemed falling from a
precipice.

Poe's private letters to his friends offer abundant
evidence that he was not insensible to the keenest
pangs of remorse. Again and again did he say to the
Demon that tracked his path, "Anathema Maranatha,"
but again and again did it return to torture and subdue.
He saw the handwriting on the wall but had no power
to avert the impending doom.

In relation to this, the fatal temptation of his life, he
says, in a letter written within a year of his death, "The ·
agonies which I have lately endured have passed my
soul through fire. Henceforth I am strong. This
those who love me shall know as well as those who
have so relentlessly sought to ruin me.   *   *   *   *
I have absolutely *no* pleasure in the stimulants in

which I sometimes so madly indulge. It has not been in the pursuit of pleasure that I have perilled life and reputation and reason. It has been in the desperate attempt to escape from torturing memories— memories of wrong and injustice and imputed dishonor —from a sense of insupportable loneliness and a dread of some strange impending doom." We believe these statements to have been sincerely uttered, and we would record here the testimony of a gentleman who, having for years known him intimately, and having been near him in his states of utter mental desolation and insanity, assured us that he had never heard from his lips a word that would have disgraced his heart or brought reproach upon his honor.

Could we believe that any plea we may have urged in extenuation of Edgar Poe's infirmities and errors would make the fatal path he trod less abhorrent to others, such would never have been proffered. No human sympathy, no human charity could avert the penalties of that erring life. One clear glance into its mournful corridors—its "halls of tragedy and chambers of retribution," would appal the boldest heart.

Theodore Parker has nobly said that "every man of genius has to hew out for himself, from the hard marbles of life, the white statue of Tranquillity." Those who have best succeeded in this sublime work will best know how to look with pity and reverent awe upon the melancholy torso which alone remains to us of Edgar Poe's misguided efforts to achieve that beautiful and august statue of Peace.

THOSE who are curious in tracing the effects of country and lineage in the mental and constitutional peculiarities of men of genius may be interested in such facts as we have been enabled to gather in relation to the ancestry of the Poet. The awakening interest in genealogical researches will make them acceptable to many readers, and in their possible influence on a character so anomalous as that of Edgar Poe they are certainly worthy of note. -

John Poe, the great-grandfather of Edgar Poe, left Ireland for America about the middle of the last century. He was of the old Norman family of Le Poer, a name conspicuous in Irish annals. Sir Roger le Poer went to Ireland, as marshal to Prince John, in the reign of Henry II., and became there the founder of a race connected with some of the most romantic and chivalrous incidents of Irish history. The heroic daring of Arnold le Poer, seneschal of Kilkenny Castle, who interposed, at the ultimate sacrifice of his liberty and his life, to save a noble lady from an ecclesiastical trial for witchcraft, the first ever instituted in the kingdom, was chronicled by Geraldus Cambrensis, and has been commemorated by recent historians.

7*

A transcript of the story, as told by Geraldus, may be found in "Ennemoser's Magic" and in "White's History of Sorcery." The bitter feuds and troubled fortunes of the Anglo-Norman settlers in Ireland are well illustrated in a recent genealogical history of the Geraldines by the Marquis of Kildare, noticed in the Edinburgh Quarterly for October 1858. The disastrous civil war of 1327, in which all the great barons of the country were involved, was occasioned by a personal feud between Arnold le Poer and Maurice of Desmond, the former having offended the dignity of the Desmond by calling him a rhymer.

The characteristics of the le Poers were marked and distinctive. They were improvident, adventurous, and recklessly brave. They were deeply involved in the Irish troubles of 1641, and when Cromwell invaded Ireland he pursued them with a special and relentless animosity. Their families were dispersed, their estates ravaged, and their lands forfeited. Of the three leading branches of the family at the time of Cromwell's invasion, Kilmaedon, Don Isle, and Curraghmore, the last only escaped his vengeance. The present representative of Curraghmore is the Marquis of Waterford. Cromwell's siege of the sea-girt castle and fortress of Don Isle, which was heroically defended by a female descendant of Nicholas le Poer, Baron of Don Isle, is, as represented by Sir Bernard Burke in his "Romance of the

Aristocracy," full of legendary interest. The beautiful domain of Powerscourt took its name from the le Poers, and was for centuries in the possession of the family. Lady Blessington, through her father, Edmund Power, claimed descent from the same old Norman family. The fact is not mentioned in Madden's memoir of the Countess, but is stated in a notice of her death published in the London Illustrated News for June 9th, 1849. The family of the le Poers, like that of the Geraldines and other Anglo-Norman settlers in Ireland, passed from Italy into the north of France, and from France through England and Wales into Ireland, where, from their isolated position and other causes, they retained for a long period their hereditary traits with far less modification from intermarriage and consociation with other races than did their English compeers. Meantime the name underwent various changes in accent and orthography. A few branches of the family still bore in Ireland the old Italian name of De la Poe.

John Poe, the great-grandfather of Edgar Poe, married a daughter of Admiral McBride, distinguished for his naval achievements and connected with some of the most illustrious families of England. From genealogical records transmitted by him to his son, David Poe, the grandfather of the poet, who was but two years of age when his parents left Ireland, it appears that different modes of spelling the name were adopted by different members of the same family. David Poe was accustomed to speak of the Chevalier le Poer, a friend of the Marquis de Grammont, as having been of his father's family. The grandfather of Edgar Poe was an officer in the Maryland line during the war of the revolution, and, as Dr Griswold has told us, the intimate friend of La Fayette. He married a lady of Pennsylvania, by the name of Cairnes, who is still remembered as having been a woman of singular beauty. The father of Edgar Poe, while a law student in the office of Wm. Gwynn, Esq., of Baltimore, married, at the age of eighteen, Elizabeth Arnold, a young English actress who was herself but a child. He first saw her at Norfolk, where he was sent on professional business, and in a few months they were married. Indignant at so imprudent a union, his parents refused their countenance to the marriage, and it was only after the birth of a child that he was forgiven and received back into the paternal mansion. During the period of his estrangement from his family he had joined his wife in a theatrical engagement. Edgar Poe was the offspring of this romantic and improvident union.

Having recorded our earnest protest against the misapprehension of his critics and the misstatements of his biographists, we leave the subject for the present, in the belief that a more impartial memoir of the poet will yet be given to the world, and the story of his sad strange life, when contemplated from a new point of view, be found—like the shield of bronze whose color was so long contested by the knights of fable—to present, at least, a silver lining.

THE END.

www.ingramcontent.com/pod-product-compliance
Lightning Source LLC
Chambersburg PA
CBHW021532270326
41930CB00008B/1212